Luisa Rose
Das Maskenfest
Ausmalbuch für Erwachsene

Bibliografische Information der Deutschen Nationalbibliothek:
Die Deutsche Nationalbibliothek verzeichnet diese Publikation in der Deutschen Nationalbibliografie; detaillierte bibliografische Daten sind im Internet über http://dnb.dnb.de abrufbar.

© 2016 Luisa Rose; 1. Auflage
Covergrafik, Texte & Illustrationen © 2016 Luisa Rose

Herstellung und Verlag: BoD – Books on Demand, Norderstedt

ISBN: 9783743113831

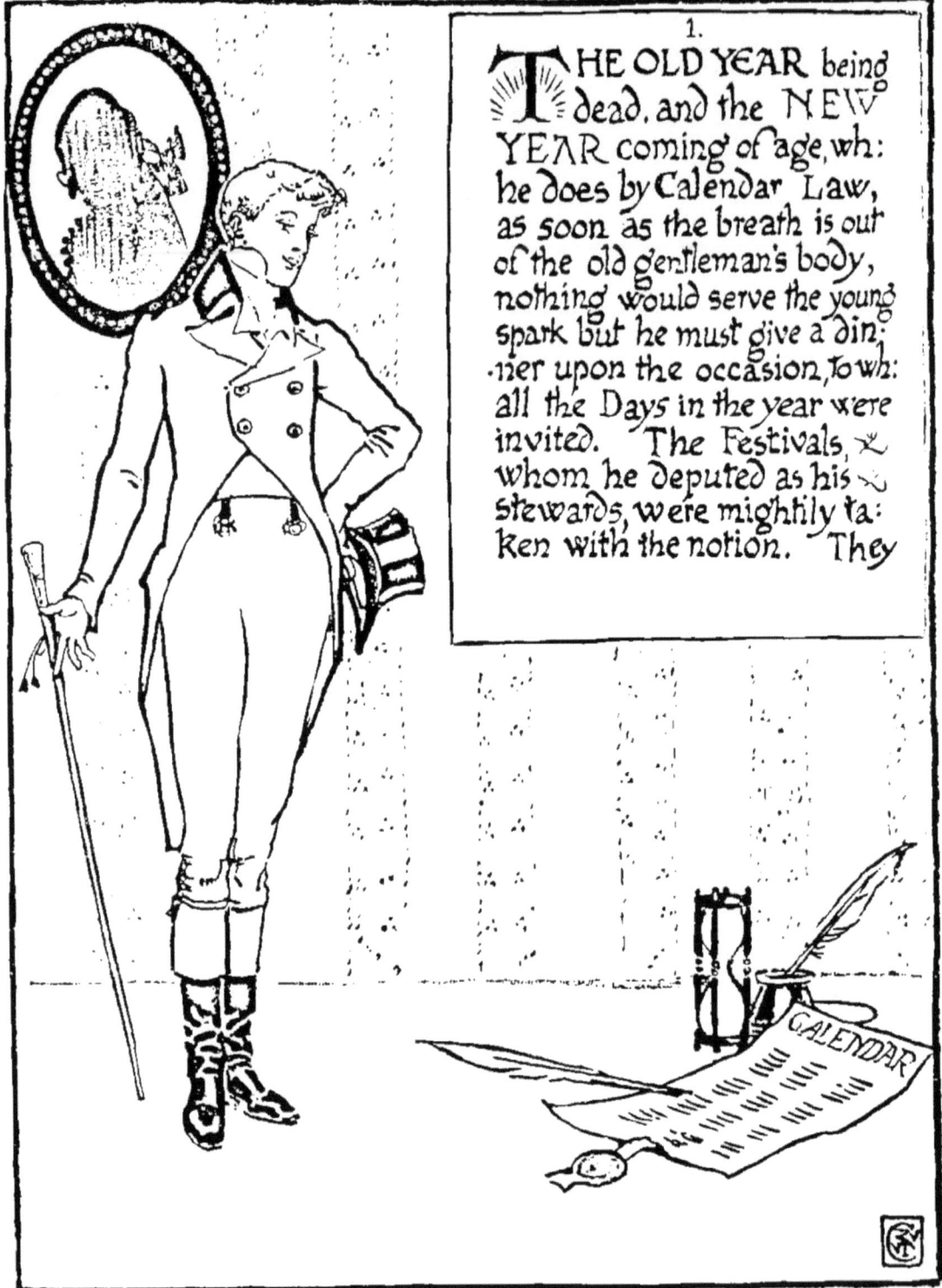

had been engaged time out of mind, they said, in providing mirth and good cheer for mortals below; and it was time they should have a taste of their own bounty. It was stiffly debated among them whether the Fasts should be admitted. Some said, the appearance of such lean, starved guests, with their mortified faces, would pervert the ends of the meeting. But the objection was overruled by Christmas Day who had a design upon Ash Wednesday

3.
(as you shall hear), and a mighty desire to see how the old Domine would behave himself in his cups.
Only the VIGILS were requested to come with their lanterns to light the

gentlefolks' home at night. ❋ · ❋ · ❋ · All the Days came to their day. Covers were provided for three hundred and sixty-five guests at the principal table; with an occasional knife and fork at the side-board for the Twenty-Ninth of February.

5.

I SHOULD have told you that cards of invitation had been issued. The carriers were THE HOURS twelve little, merry whirligig foot-pages, as you should desire to see, that went all round, and found

what scornful. Yet some said, TWELFTH DAY cut her out and out, for she came in a tiffany suit, white and gold, like a queen on a frost-cake, all roy:=al glittering, and Epiphanous.

Rainy Days came in, dripping; and sun-shiny Days helped them to change their stockings

Wedding Day was there in his marriage finery, a little the worse for wear.

12

Pay Day came late, as he always does; and Dooms-day sent word— he might be expected

April Fool (as my young lord's jester) took upon himself to marshal the guests, and wild work he made with it. It would have posed old Erra Pater to have found out any given Day in the year, to erect a scheme upon—

14

good Days, bad Days were so shuffled together, to the confounding of all sober horoscopy.   He had stuck the Twenty-First of June next to the Twenty-Second of December, and the former looked like a Maypole siding a marrow-bone.

15

Ash Wednesday got wedged in (as was concerted) betwixt Christmas & Lord Mayor's Days. Lord! how he laid about him! Nothing but barons of beef & turkeys would go down with him to the great greasing & detriment of his new sack-cloth bib & tucker. And still Christmas Day was at his elbow, plying him with the wassail-bowl, till he roared, & hiccupp'd, & protested there was no faith in dried ling, * * * a sour, windy, acrimonious, censorious hy-po-crit-crit-critical mess & no dish for a gentleman. Then he dipt his fist into the middle of the great custard that stood before his left-hand neighbour, & daubed his hungry beard all over with it, till you would have taken him for the Last Day in December it so hung in icicles.

AT another part of the table, Shrove Tuesday was helping the Second of September to some cock broth,—

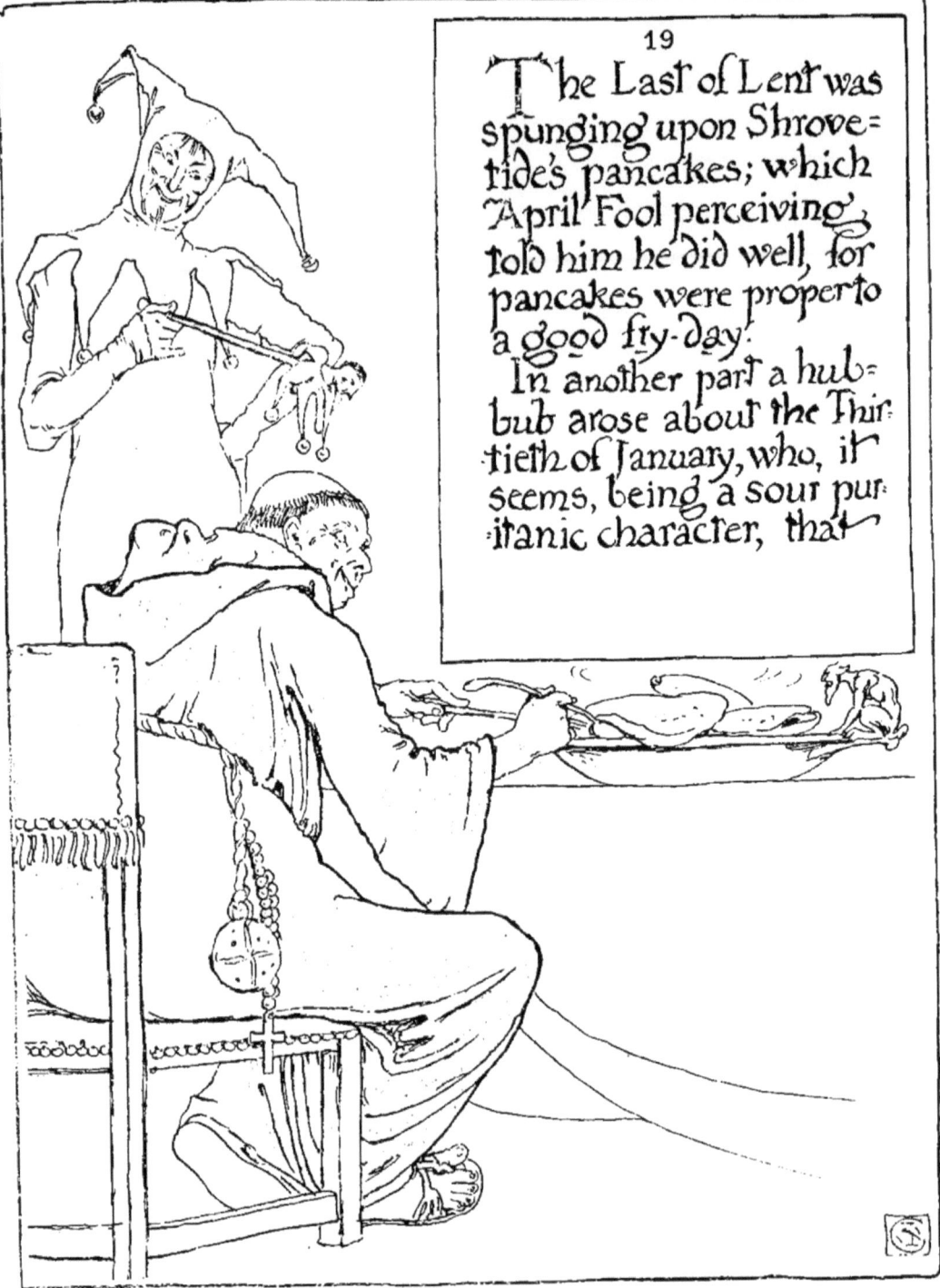

The Last of Lent was spunging upon Shrovetide's pancakes; which April Fool perceiving, told him he did well, for pancakes were proper to a good fry-day.

In another part a hubbub arose about the Thirtieth of January, who, it seems, being a sour puritanic character, that

thought nobody's meat good or sanctified enough for him, had smuggled into the room a calf's head which he had had cooked at home for that purpose, thinking to feast thereon incontinently; but as it lay in the dish March Many weathers, who is a very fine lady, and subject to the meagrims, screamed

out there was a "human head in the platter," and raved about Herodias' daughter to that degree, that the obnoxious viand was obliged to be removed; nor did she recover her stomach till she

22

had gulped down a Restorative, confected of Oak Apple, which the merry Twenty-Ninth of May always carries about with him for that purpose.

24

August grew hot upon the matter, affirming time out of mind the prescriptive right to have lain with her, till her rival basely supplanted her;

* * * * *

April Fool being made mediator, confirmed the right in the strongest form of words to the appellant, but decided for peace' sake that the exercise of it should remain with the present possessor.

* * * * *

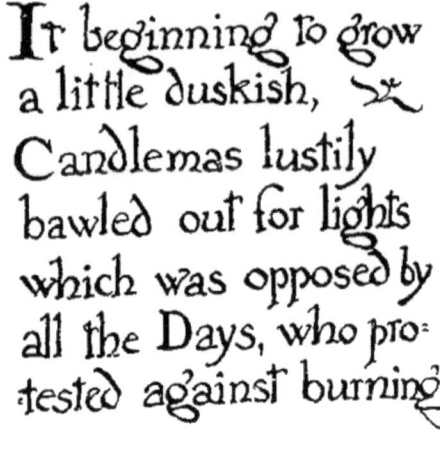

It beginning to grow a little duskish, Candlemas lustily bawled out for lights which was opposed by all the Days, who protested against burning daylight. Then fair water was handed round in silver ewers, and the same lady was observed to take an unusual time in washing herself.

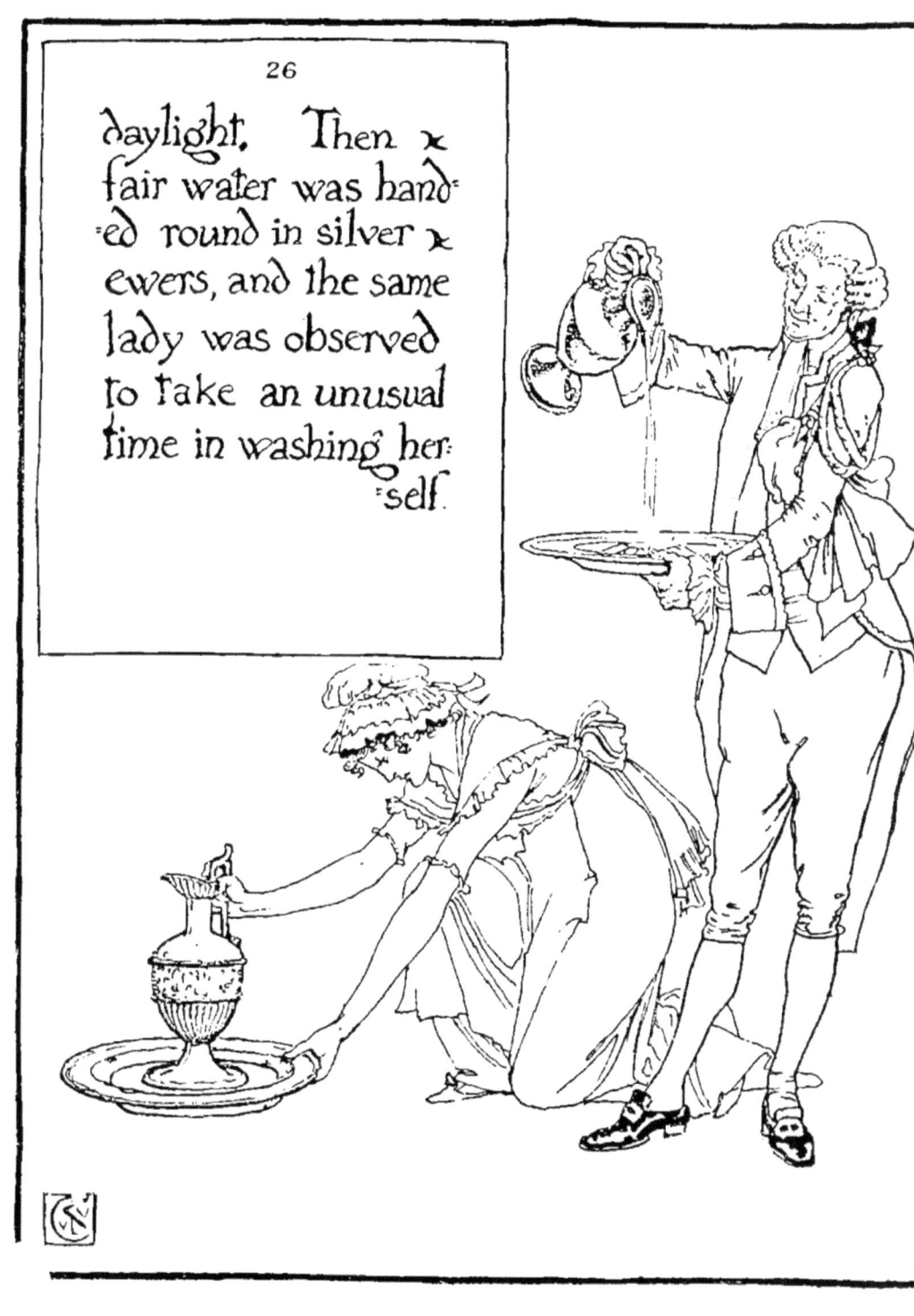

May-Day, with that sweetness which is peculiar to her, in a neat speech proposing the health of the founder, crowned her goblet (and by her example the rest of the company) with garlands. This being done, the lordly New Year from the upper end of the table,

28

in a cordial but somewhat lofty tone, returned thanks. He felt proud on an occasion of meeting so many of his father's late tenants, promised to improve their farms, & at the same time to abate {if anything was found unreasonable} in their rents.

At the mention of this the Four Quarter Days involuntarily looked at each other, & smiled; April Fool whistled to an old tune of "New Brooms" & a surly old rebel at the further end of the table {who was discovered to be no other than the Fifth of November} muttered out distinctly enough to be heard by the whole com=

pany, words to this effect; that "when the old one is gone, he is a fool that looks for a better." This rudeness of his, the guests resenting, unanimously voted his expulsion; & the malcontent was thrust out neck & heels into the cellar, as the properest place for such a boute-feu & firebrand as he had shewn himself to be.

33

Shrove tide, Lord Mayor's Day, and April Fool, next joined in a glee — Which is the properest day to drink? in which all the days chiming in, made a merry burden.

They next fell to quibbles & conumdrums.

34

he question being proposed, who had the greatest number of followers — the Quarter Days said, there could be no question as to that; for they had all the creditors in the world dogging their heels. April Fool gave it in favour of the Forty Days before Easter; because the debtors in all cases outnumbered the creditors, & they kept lent all the year round.

All this while Valentine's Day kept courting pretty May, who sate next him, slipping amorous billets-doux un=

36

-der the table, till the Dog Days {who are naturally of a warm constitution} began to bark and rage exceedingly.

Weitere Ausmalbücher von Luisa Rose:

Titel	ISBN
Alice im Wunderland	9783741297502
Blumen und Märchen	9783743102002
Der Struwwelpeter	9783743102699
Die Struwwelliese	9783743102811
Don Quixote	9783743104037
Drei kleine Schweine	9783743104099
Eine Blumenhochzeit	9783743104105
Fröhliche Reigenspiele	9783743104112
Lustige Tanzspiele	9783743104273
Reise ins antike Griechenland	9783743112568
Flucht ins antike Griechenland	9783743112599
Pariser Leben im 19.Jahrhundert	9783743112704
Die Sommerkönigin	9783743112742
Der Schneider und die Krähe	9783743112827
Die Wikinger	9783743113275
Hänsel und Gretel	9783743114265
Max und Moritz	9783743103214
Schnurrdirburr	9783743112834
Mode des 18. und 19. Jahrhunderts	9783743112971
Kostümbilder des 18. und 19. Jahrhunderts	9783743114401
Abenteuer im Bienenland	9783743117051
Griechische Helden der Antike	9783743117709
Märchen alter Zeit	9783743116559

Notizbücher von Luisa Rose:

Titel	ISBN
Drachentöter (Notizbuch)	9783743113077
Natures Wonders (Notizbuch)	9783743113817
Gedankenspiel Notizen (Notizbuch)	9783743113886
Smaragd Notizen (Notizbuch)	9783743114296
Jagd Notizen (Notizbuch)	9783743114302
Tradition (Notizbuch)	9783743114319
Antik Notizbuch (Notizbuch)	9783743114326
Veni Vidi Vici (Notizbuch)	9783743114340
Black List (Notizbuch)	9783743114371
Mystic Notes (Notizbuch)	9783743114388
Magic Notes (Notizbuch)	9783743114418
Fantasien (Notizbuch)	9783743114463
Creative Notes (Notizbuch)	9783743114487
Persönliche Notizen (Notizbuch)	9783743114494
Peter Pan (Notizbuch)	9783743114531
Rose (Notizbuch)	9783743114548
Quality Street (Notizbuch)	9783743114555
Rubin Notizen (Notizbuch)	9783743114647
Schmetterlinge (Notizbuch)	9783743114661
Ali Baba (Notizbuch)	9783743114678
The portrait of a Lady (Notizbuch)	9783743114692
Shakespeare (Notizbuch)	9783743114722
Brainstorming (Notizbuch)	9783743114739
Merlin (Notizbuch)	9783743114746
Rügen (Notizbuch)	9783743114784

Möchtest du über neue Bücher von Luisa Rose per email Informiert werden? Dann schicke eine Email mit ‚Newsletter' im Betreff an Luisa.Rose@t-online.de